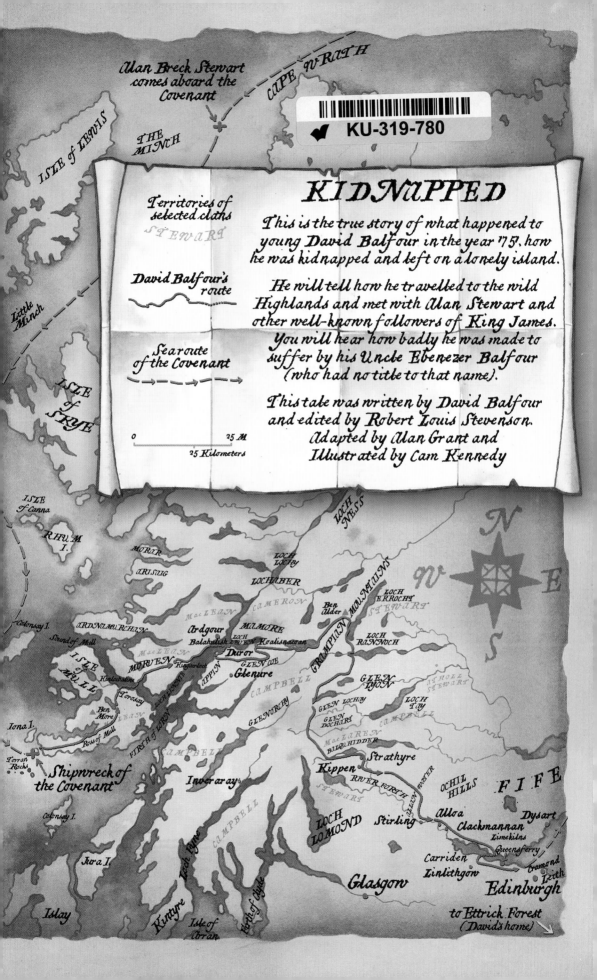

I was only 17 and excited by the idea that I had a rich relation.

Should I go?

Yes - I would!

I was on my own now. I was going from my dull country life to live in a grand house full of people.

I took a last look at my village and the trees that grew over my parents' graves.

Then I set out for the House of Shaws to meet my rich relative.

It was on the morning of the next day that I got to the top of a hill and saw the city of Edinburgh below me and beyond that the sea. Black smoke rose from the city.

I was amazed to see so clearly the flag on the castle and the great ships on the water.

At dusk I met a mean-looking woman.

There's the House of Shaws. Blood built it and blood stopped the building of it.

And blood will bring it down.

If you see the Laird tell him Jennet curses him and his house.

Black be their fall.

I had my father's letter and must go on. But I was thinking hard...

Was this the place I was looking for?

Was it here that I would meet new friends and make my fortune?

The room was almost bare. On the table were a bowl of porridge, a bone spoon and a cup of ale.

Give me your father's letter.

You know my father?

I do indeed, for he was my brother.

So you see, David, I am your uncle.

I was amazed. My father never said he had a brother. I ate the bowl of thin porridge while he read the letter.

So you hoped to find a rich relation, did you?

I am not poor or asking for help.

Hoot-toot! Don't be angry with me. We'll get on fine. Now go to bed.

Can I have a light, Uncle?

No lights in this house. I'm too afraid of a fire.

He shut the door and locked me in. What sort of old miser was this uncle of mine?

In the morning light, I saw that 20 years ago this room must have been attractive.

But no one had looked after it, and now it was a filthy mess.

My uncle seemed to live off porridge and weak beer.

You've made it clear you don't want me here. Even if I am family, I had better go.

Hoot-toot! Stay a day or two. I'll do the right thing by you, you'll see.

I spent some time in the old library...

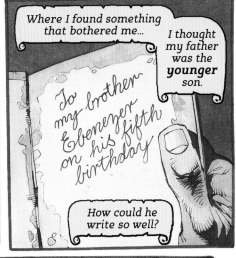

Where I found something that bothered me...

I thought my father was the **younger** son.

To my brother Ebenezer on his fifth birthday

How could he write so well?

When I asked my uncle about it...

Were you and my father **twins** by any chance?

Eh? Eh?

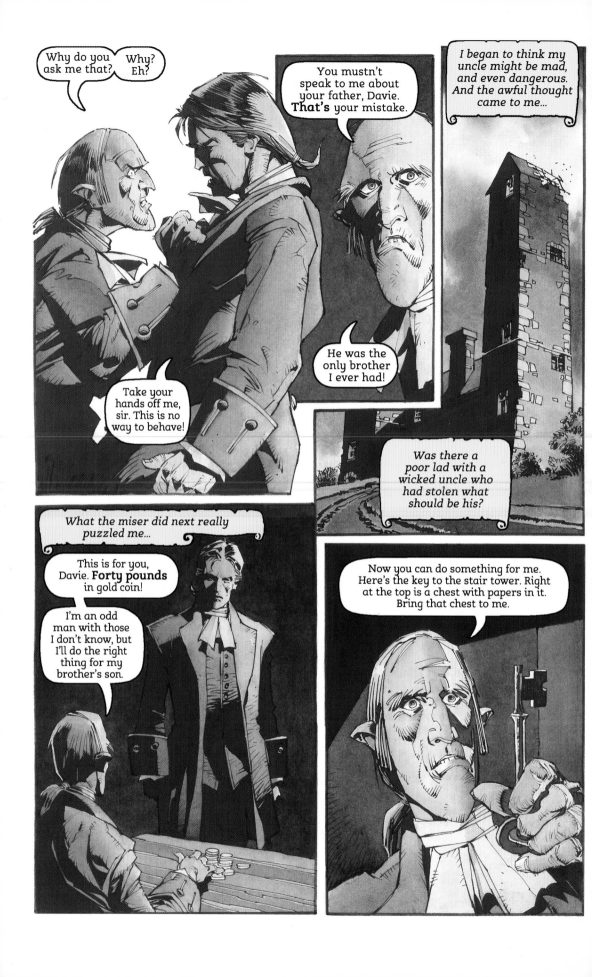

I was very angry. As I felt my way down, the storm broke.

There he is - waiting for the sound of my fall!

There was a great clap of thunder. My uncle ran inside in a panic.

I came up close behind him and suddenly put my hands on his shoulders...

Ah-ha!

Eeek!

D-D-Davie! Are you alive? Oh, man, are you alive?

Yes, I am - no thanks to you!

Why give me money - then try to kill me? Why are you so scared of me?

- I'll tell you everything, Davie. In the morning.

It's my heart, you see. I'm feeling very weak!

I locked him in his room and made up a bigger fire than had been seen in the kitchen for years.

I sat there till late at night, thinking about this ruined House of Shaws.

Next morning, I begged him to answer me. But...

Hoot-toot, Davie! Let me finish my porridge.

He was trying to think up some cunning lie when there was a knock at the door.

You stay where you are, sir. I'll go.

How are you, mate?

I have a letter from old Heasy-Oasy to Mr Balfour.

And, I say, mate, I'm **hungry**.

Starving!

Listen to this, Davie!

My partner, Captain Hoseason, wants me to come to the Queen's Ferry.

If you come with me, we can visit a lawyer, Mr Rankeillor. He was a friend of your father's.

My uncle would not dare to harm me in the busy harbour. And I was keen to meet a lawyer - one who knew my father, too.

Very well.

Let's go!

They call me Ransome, mate.

I've been a sea-dog since I was a little boy.

Captain Heasy-Oasy's a hard man, but no sailor. It's Mr Shuan, the first mate, that sails the boat.

And when he's drunk, he beats the hell out of me.

He'll be sorry one day, you'll see.

I've killed a man before, you know. More than one!

But there are some worse off than me.

There's the twenty-pounders... Men who've been kidnapped to be sold as slaves in America!

Soon, Captain Hoseason himself came to see me...

Your uncle speaks well of you, David. You must have a drink with me on my ship.

I'm sorry, Captain. I have to see the lawyer, Rankeillor.

Take care, lad. Your uncle means to do you harm!

Come aboard my ship till I can speak to you alone.

I thought I had found a friend who would help me.

So, like a fool, I went in the boat with them.

The Captain and I were the first up and onto the ship...

But where's my uncle?

Well, that's just it, lad.

The boat was going back to shore...

I've been tricked!

Help! Help!

My uncle was looking evil and afraid.

Strong hands grabbed me and pulled me back...

I saw a blinding flash as I was struck down...

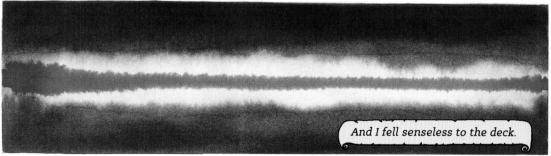

And I fell senseless to the deck.

I came to in the dark. I was in great pain. The ship was rolling madly up and down. The sea roared and the sailors shouted.

It took me a long time to work out that I was lying deep down inside that awful ship, that we were at sea and a gale was blowing.

A great gloom fell on me. How stupid I had been! I was so angry at my uncle, who had betrayed me.

I must have lain there for days before the first mate came with the Captain to have a look at me.

You were paid to take him to America, Captain.

If you keep him here, it will be murder!

I was put in the bows with the other men. I began to get better.

The sailors were a rough lot. Some had been pirates, others were deserters from the King's Navy.

But, for the most part, they were not evil - except for the drunken Mr Shuan.

You filthy brat! You need a good beating!

But Shuan was the only one of them who really knew how to sail.

They needed him, so no one would stand up to him.

I tried to be a friend to Ransome, but he was hardly human.

Oh 'tis my delight on a shiny night In the season of the year!

I don't remember my father. I think he made clocks. We had a bird, a starling, with a pretty call.

Don't you want to find your father? To go home?

The sea's my home now, and the wind, and my jug of beer.

All this time the ship was blown back by the wind and tossed by the sea. Everyone was hard at work.

It was a week later and I was even more unhappy.

I was very upset about poor Ransome. And soon I would be sold as a slave. What's more, the ship was an unlucky one...

On the tenth night, there was the awful sound of splintering wood and men yelling in despair...

For pity's sake! They've run us down!

Someone's still alive!

Throw him a rope! We can still save him!

The Captain left - in a hurry, I thought. I was alone with the stranger...

So... You are a rebel, sir?

Yes. And you, I think, are a King's man.

Well, Mr King's Man, this bottle is empty.

I pay 60 guineas and there's not a drop left!

I'll ask the Captain for more.

I heard low voices in the fog.

We can come at him from both sides and grab him by the arms.

We can stab him before he can draw his sword!

David! This wild Highland man is a danger to the ship and an enemy to our King.

You must get us pistols from the Roundhouse. And we'll share some of his gold with you.

Very well, sirs.

I'll do it.

But I was very angry with these greedy, disloyal men. I was not going to help them.

Do you want to be killed?

Eh? What are you saying?

They're all murderers here! They've killed a boy already - now it's your turn!

Well, they haven't got me yet.

Will you stand by me, lad?

I'm not a thief, or a murderer. I'll stand by you. I'm David Balfour.

Of Shaws.

My name is Stewart - a king's name. But they call me Alan Breck.

We took out cutlasses and pistols from the store...

There are 15 against us!

I will guard the main door, David. You must take the rest.

I warn you, Alan, I'm not a good shot!

Then don't fire to **this** side! I would rather have 10 enemies in front of me than one friend like you shooting at my back!

The ship was badly off now, without Mr Shuan's skills as a sailor.

We were somewhere off the coast of Mull when...

There's rocks off our bow!

That's the Torran Rocks. They say they're ten miles long!

We'll have to take our chances!

Next moment we struck the rocks with a crash that threw us flat on deck...

Alan! Help me get the boat out and we may yet live!

What's the point? The islands of Mull and Earraid are Campbell country! I'm a dead man there!

Suddenly a huge wave knocked the ship over. I lost my hold and was thrown over the rail and into the sea...

For pity's sake!

David!

I clung in panic to a broken spar...

Help!
Help!

But the ship was gone.

As I was washed ashore, I thought I had never seen a place so lonely and bare as this island of Earraid.

Next morning...

Which way to Torosay, my friend?

No English! Go away! No English!

So I let my money speak for me...

And suddenly the man could talk...

Torosay?

Why, it's not far at all. I'll take you there myself and it'll only cost you five shillings!

We walked for miles in silence, then...

I'll need five shillings more now, or you can find your own way!

Why, you dirty cheat!

You'll pay up, one way or another!

But I was a strong lad, and very angry...

Perhaps, sir, that will teach you to keep your word from now on!

It took me four days to get from Earraid to Torosay, some 50 miles. But at last I was sitting in the ferry of Alan's kinsman, Neil Roy McRob.

In the mouth of Loch Aline, a great ship was at anchor, ready to sail with people bound for the American colonies.

When men like the Red Fox got no rent from these people, they stole their lands and sold the unhappy families into slavery.

In all my travels, I never saw such a cruel, sad sight.

When we got to land, I showed my silver button to Neil Roy...

Alan said you'd come. He's told me what you must do.

Alan had planned my journey. I was to reach Ardgour the next day, and spend the night with John of the Claymore.

Two days later I would cross the loch at Balachulish, then find my way to James of the Glens at Aucharn in Appin.

So, at last, I came to Appin, close to the wood of Lettermore.

It was here that I was attacked twice over, first by a cloud of stinging midges...

And then by the fear that I was doing the wrong thing. Why was I following the outlaw Alan Breck? Why hadn't I set out for Edinburgh on my own?

Had I gone mad?

I ran as hard as I could...

Then, amazed, I heard a voice...

Creep in here, in the bushes!

Alan! Alan Breck!

It's no time for greetings, Davie!

For your life, lad - follow me!

The pace was killing, and it seemed as if my heart would explode. But Alan did not slow down, and I made myself keep up with him.

At last, high in the woods, we rested a while, and I could tell Alan my fear...

I like you very much, Alan - but I cannot have any part in such a vile murder!

As one friend to another, Mr Balfour of Shaws...

If I were going to kill someone, I would do it on my own land, where my kinsmen would suffer for it.

And I would carry a sword or a gun, and not a fishing rod on my back!

They'll be after both of us now.

We must run!

I'm not afraid of the law of my own country.

Davie, Davie! You know nothing.

A Campbell has been killed. The trial will be at Inverara, the Campbell capital. The judge and jury will be Campbells.

We'll meet the same end as the Red Fox did down by that road!

You must escape to the moors with me as an outlaw, or you'll hang like a dog!

If you put it like that, I have no choice!

As we travelled, Alan told me how the ship had sunk, and how he had got away from Hoseason and the other men who escaped the sea.

Alan's plan had been to hide in James of the Glen's home. But the murder of the Red Fox had changed all that.

There will be Redcoats all around here tomorrow! We must travel on.

They fed us and clothed us, but...

We are in a bad mess, Alan.

You and I are kinsmen. If they look for you, they will look for me. All I can do is...

Put a reward on your head!

Alan's money had been sent ahead of us. We took our swords and pistols with us, and some oats and brandy. There were rewards out for us. It was time to head for the moors.

This place is no good for you and me, Davie. They're sure to look for us here!

Come on!

The leap before us was far wider and I was scared to death...

I can't do it, Alan! I dare not jump again!

Drink this, Davie – for you must jump!

And then Alan had jumped...

Hang or drown Davie!

And luckily for us,
we were just in time.

When night falls,
we'll slip down past
them and get away.

And what
shall we do
till then?

Bake, Davie. We're
going to bake like
cakes in the sun!

Cluny had found copies of our 'Wanted' papers.

It says Alan Breck is "a small active man with a pitted face. He wears French clothes. With him is a tall, strong lad, about 18, with no beard."

I'd had food and drink, but I still felt weak and ill. I went to bed. Alan and Cluny played cards.

I woke, and slept, and slept, and woke. It all seemed a strange dream...

David, lend me your money, will you? All right, lad?

All – all right...

When at last I felt better, it was to find...

You shouldn't have lent me your money, Davie! I'm a fool when it comes to cards!

I've lost the lot – and my own gold, too!

To end this miserable tale, Cluny gave me back my share of the money, but he wasn't happy.

When Alan and I left his Cage, we were hardly speaking to each other.

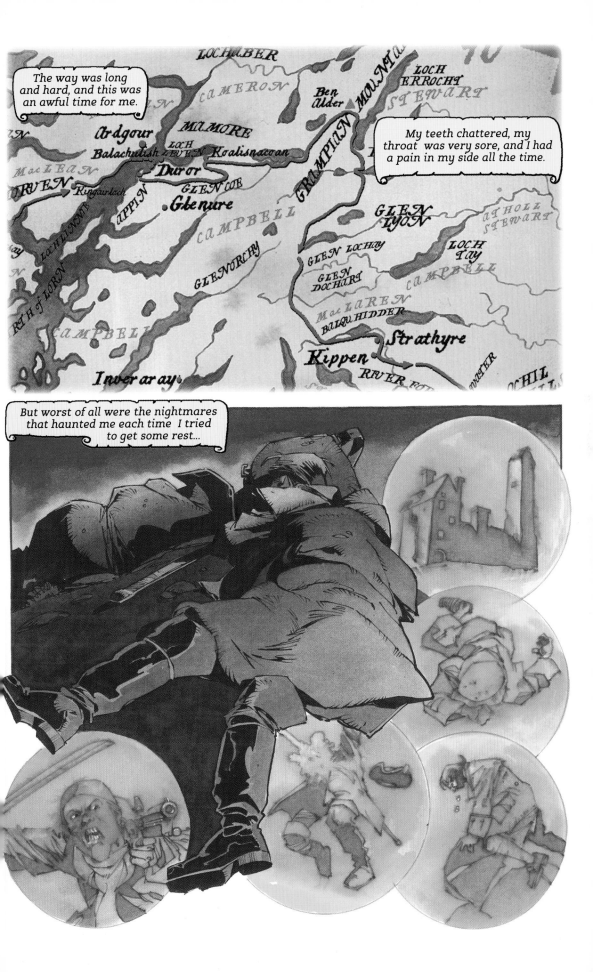

We stayed for almost a month at the home of a MacLaren in Balquhidder. A doctor came and looked after me all the time.

It was late August when we set off again. We had hardly any money left. We had to find the lawyer, Rankeillor.

The bridge at Stirling was manned by Redcoats. So Alan found a boat to take us over the water...

And at long last, I came home to the Lowlands.

The plan was that Alan should hide near Newhalls. I would go to the harbour to look for my uncle's lawyer, Rankeillor.

I told him my whole story, from when I left my village to my travels in the Highlands. I told him the many ways that my uncle had betrayed me.

Tut tut! To have his own nephew kidnapped!

But when I spoke of Alan Breck...

I'm a lawyer, David. I can't involve myself with outlaws.

If you must talk about one, give him a false name...

Why not Mr Thomson?

Shaws is yours for certain, David. But if your uncle won't admit it, how can we prove it?

I think I have a plan, sir, that will make my uncle confess his sins.

But I'll need the help of my friend... Mr Thomson!

Rankeillor came with me to Newhalls, and I gave the signal that I had agreed with Alan.

We told Alan – or should I say Mr Thomson – of the plan. Then all three of us set off to play out the last act.

It was dark when we got to the House of Shaws. There was not a light to be seen.

Rankeillor and I crept softly up and hid beside the corner of the house...

While Alan began to knock very loudly on the door.

Ebenezer Balfour! I need to speak to you!

Then how much will you pay? What did you pay Hoseason to kidnap the lad?

£20. And another £20 when he'd sold the lad in the Colonies.

Thank you, Mr Balfour. You have confessed everything!

Rankeillor!

Oh, saints alive! D-D-David!

Goo[d] eveni[ng] Uncl[e]

Come, come, Mr Ebenezer, no need for gloom. We'll make a good deal with you!

And so we did. Uncle Ebenezer would give me two thirds of his income from Shaws. So I, the poor lad, had come home, and now I was rich. I had a name in the country.

Next day, Alan and I set out slowly on our way. We didn't much want to walk, or talk. Soon we had to part, and the memory of all we had been through together made us sad.

We came over the hill of Costorphine and looked down on the bogs and over to the city and the castle on the hill. We knew that our ways must part here.

It was almost noon when I passed the West Kirk and the Grassmarket and walked into Edinburgh. Rankeillor had set up a credit for me to draw out the money that would take Alan safely to France.

The tall houses, the narrow doorways, the noise and endless activity... all this shocked and confused me...

So I simply went with the crowd.

But all the time I was thinking of Alan at Costorphine.

And all the time I felt cold inside, as if I was to blame for something that was wrong.

As I drifted along, I ended up, by good luck, at the door of the bank where I had a credit to draw out the money.

the end